Begin with large dots and use them as a guideline. These smaller dots are too close together.

Here the dots are evenly spaced but too far apart.

Here dots are spaced evenly and the letter is easy to read.

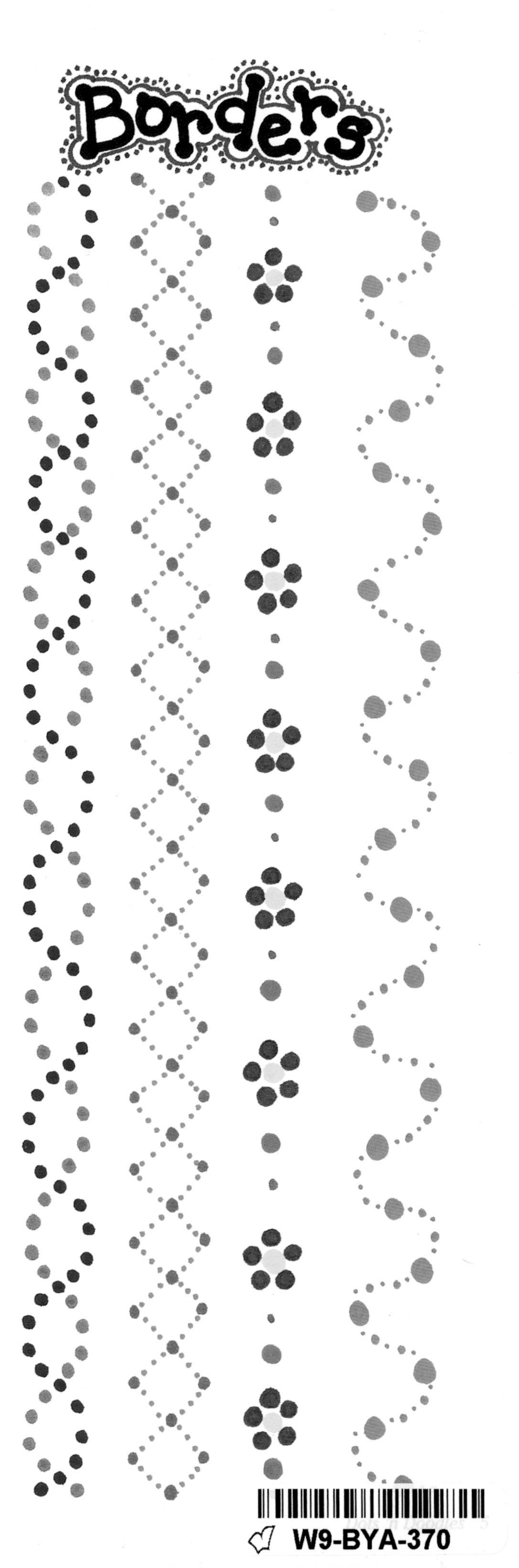

W9-BYA-370

Dots & Dashes
Step 1
Flower
Step 1
Music
Step 1
Step 2
Anchor
Step 1
Step 2
Spider
Step 1
Cat
Step 1
Pumpkin
Step 1
Step 2
Branch
Step 1
Step 2
Tree
Step 1
Holly
a b c d e f g h i
j k l m n o p q r
s t u v w x y z !
ABCDEFGHIJ
KLMNOPQRS
TUVWXYZ!

Layout & Design

PERSONALIZING ON PAPER turns simple paper projects into cherished possessions. Stationery, cards, invitations, album pages and certificates become unique keepsakes with the addition of names and individual designs.

PERSONALIZING TIPS & HINTS

DOTS 'N DOODLES includes dozens of designs and alphabets for making your personalizing projects quick, easy and fun.

1. Trace designs and transfer them to your project with graphite paper.

2. For clear glass or plastic pieces, make a black and white copy and tape it behind the area to be painted.

3. Enlarge or reduce the patterns on a copy machine to fit your project.

4. Combine designs and alphabets. Use the ideas on any surface you want to personalize. The possibilities are limitless.

TIP: With practice you will find it easy and fast to copy designs free-hand.

Table of Contents

MANY THANKS to my friends for their cheerful help and wonderful ideas!
Art Coordinator-Kathy McMillan
Art Director-Laurie Rice
Artist-Janet Long
Photography-David & Donna Thomason

Suzanne McNeill

Dot Designs!

1 Dot
SUN

2 Dots
CHERRIES

3 Dots
FLOWER

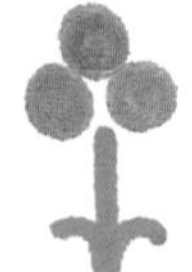

4 Dots
BUG

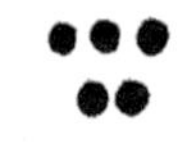

5 Dots
FLOWER

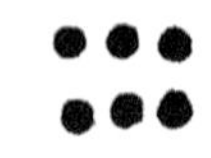

6 Dots
FLOWER

7 Dots
GRAPES

8 Dots
FLOWER

9 Dots
CATERPILLAR

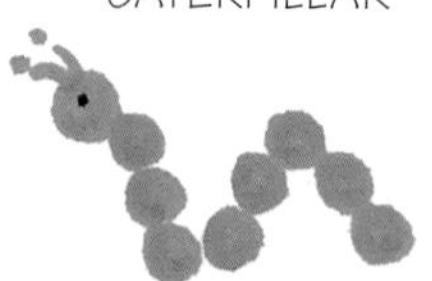

10 Dots
COOKIE

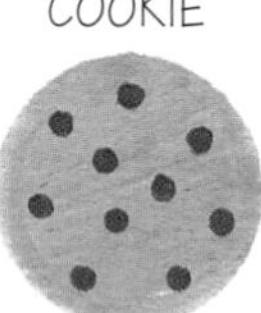

11 Dots
FLOWER

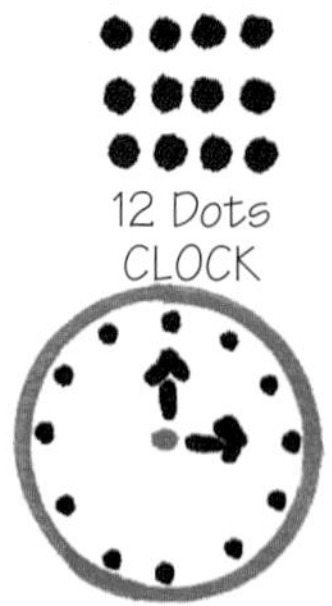
12 Dots
CLOCK

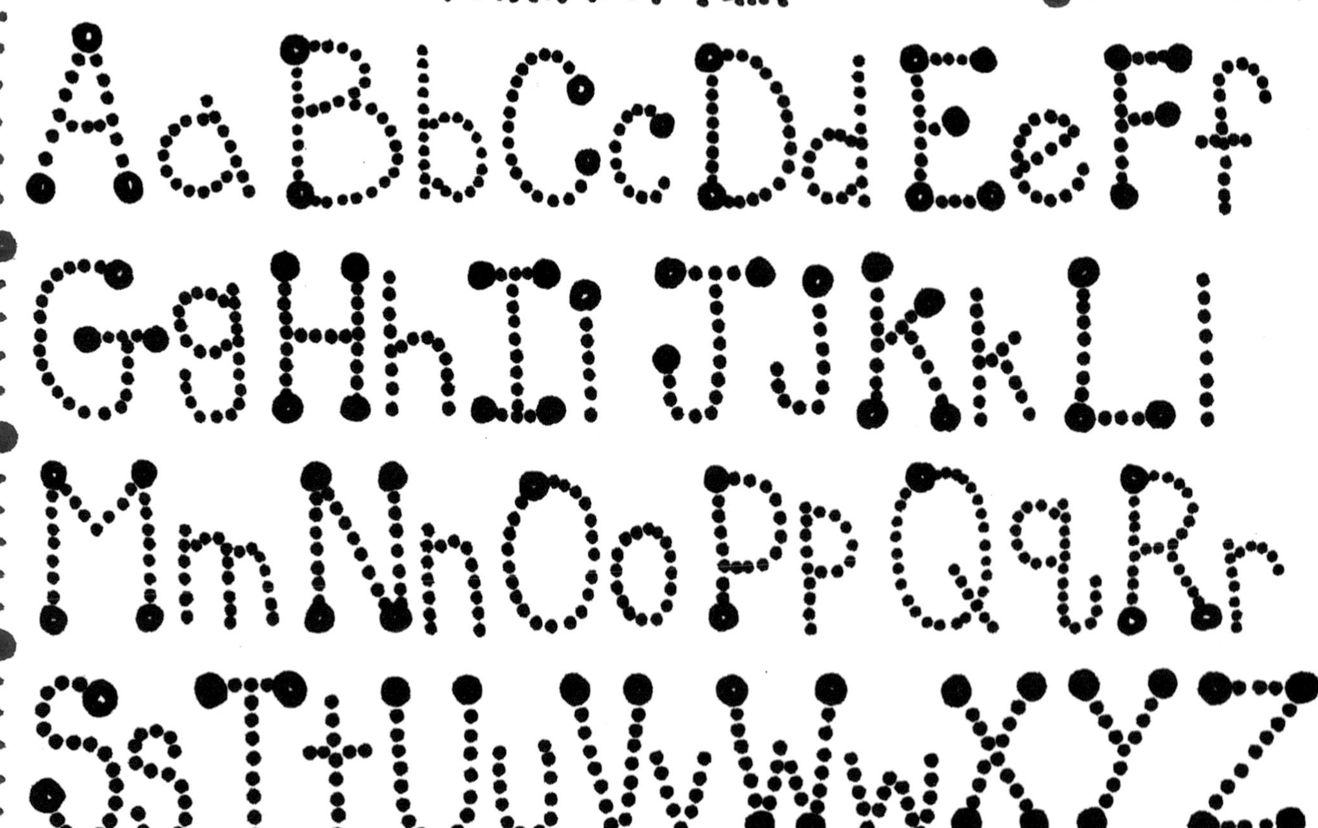

1. Use a ruler or place masking tape for a guide to make straight lines a breeze.
2. Practice drawing your designs on paper first to get the feel of the marker.
3. Always shake your Paint Pen marker and tap it on a scrap of paper before writing. This will prevent blobs and will start an even flow before you begin.
4. If you are going to use one color on top of another color as with the swirl on the sun, be sure to allow the first color to dry completely before adding the second. This will prevent bleeding.

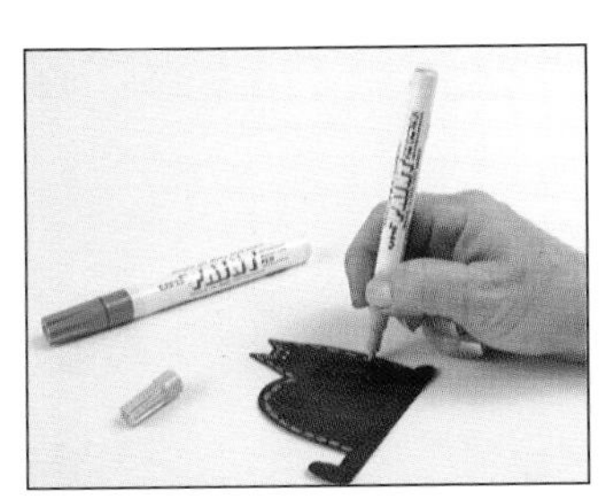

Tip: Hold paint pens perpendicular to the surface to keep lines even in width and to achieve a consistent paint flow.

Tip: Holding paint pens at a 45° angle (like writing with a pencil or ballpoint pen) may cause paint to flow unevenly.

Slashes & Swirls

Celebrate Your Baby's "Firsts"

An adorable milestones page helps keep memories of your baby's first smile, first steps, or first tooth fresh for generations to come. Even if you can't snap a picture of each magical moment, your loving descriptions of those fabulous firsts will bring your little one's achievements to life.

You Will Need:

- *2 sheets (12" x 12") white cardstock*
- *2 sheets (12" x 12") grass patterned paper*
- *1 sheet (8½" x 11") floral paper*
- *1 sheet (5" x 7") each: speckled gray paper, gray cardstock, tan cardstock*
- *1 set flower stickers*
- *Basics: black pen, alphabet lettering stencil, fine-tip scissors, & adhesive*

Fun With Photos Memories & More™ presented by ➤

Milestones page design by Jennifer McLaughlin. *Magical Milestones* page by Lisa Bearnson with photos by Becky Higgins.

Start by sorting through your photos to find your favorite firsts. Following are tips for jazzing up your photos, writing memorable descriptions, and decorating the white cardstock background of this two-page scrapbook album spread.

✪ **PHOTOS** Trim away any distracting photographic elements to bring your baby into focus. You can even frame one or two photos for more impact. Here, we cut out "grass" frames and layered slightly smaller floral frames on top of them.

✪ **DECORATIVE ACCENTS** Cut a piece of grass paper in half; trim it to create a lawn for the bottom of page. Use extra paper for additional accents, such as grass blades. Cut stones from gray paper and cardstock, and tan cardstock (patterns at right).

✪ **TITLE** You can trace letters on grass pattern paper, cut out, and set aside. Or, you can pencil the letters on the white background cardstock. *Tip: Use a store-bought alphabet stencil to trace the letters.*

✪ **DESCRIPTION** Practice writing about the milestones, such as "first smile," on scrap paper before writing directly on your cardstock. *Tip: Note the date or age for each milestone.*

Finish by arranging photos and accents on the cardstock, leaving room for your written descriptions. Use the scrapbook pages on the front of this card for inspiration. Adhere items, and pencil in descriptions. Trace over text with black marker.

Make It Mine!

NO PHOTOS? NO PROBLEM!

You can take pictures of your child at a "milestone" age (such as six months or one year), and reflect on the achievements to that date.

FAVORITE FIRSTS

Babies grow so quickly, it seems they have "firsts" every day. Here are a few activities that you might want to record:

- First bath
- First smile
- Rolling over
- Sitting up
- Crawling
- First tooth
- Standing
- First steps
- First words
- Tasting new foods
- First haircut

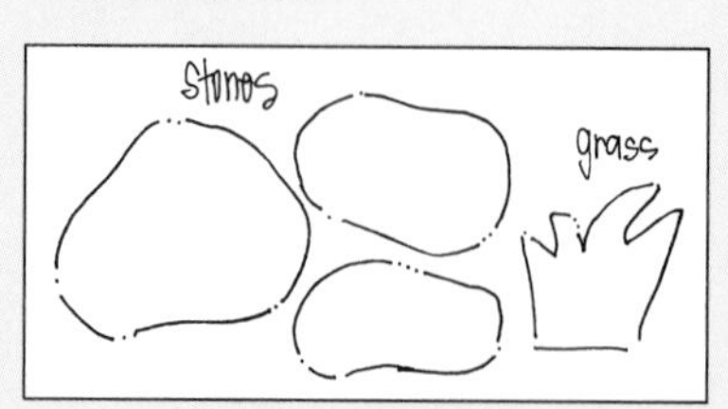

ROCK PATTERN

If you're having trouble creating rock and grass accents, you can photocopy these patterns (try enlarging them 150%), and cut them out. Use them to trace as many shapes as you need!

Fun with Photos, Memories & More is a trademark of IMP AB.
For questions please call 1-800-416-1355. www.imp-usa.com
Printed in USA 10908 20038 1016 Pack 00(r)

©MMIII PRIMEDIA Special Interest Publications Inc.
Produced by International Masters Publishers Inc. under license.
Creating Keepsakes® is a registered trademark of PRIMEDIA Inc.

the Good list

Better together

Certain things in life are just meant to go hand in hand. Check out our favorite pairs. *by Holly Crawford*

1. Peanut butter and jelly

2. T-shirt and jeans
3. Baseball games and hot dogs
4. Manicure and pedicure
5. Little girls and velvet dresses
6. Churches and stained glass
7. Ballet flats and capris

8. Men and muscles

9. Laverne and Shirley
10. Strawberries and chocolate
11. Laptops and Starbucks
12. Big brothers and little sisters
13. Misery and company
14. J. K. Rowling and a rainy day
15. Treadmills and iPods

16. Wet grass and bare feet

17. Santa Claus and chimneys
18. Carrie B. and Mr. Big
19. Pork chops and applesauce
20. Sunglasses and convertibles
21. Chocolate brown and pink
22. Weddings and white
23. Coffee and the Sunday paper
24. S'mores and campfires

25. Stars and stripes

26. Porches and rocking chairs
27. Cotton candy and carnivals
28. Airplanes and magazines
29. Sixty-five degrees and sunny
30. Grandma and Grandpa
31. Popcorn and movie previews
32. Ray Charles and Georgia
33. Cupcakes and sprinkles

34. Hugs and kisses

35. Teddy bears and toddlers
36. Tomato soup and grilled cheese
37. Husbands and La-Z-Boys
38. Snowy nights and fireplaces

39. Green eggs and ham

40. Yearbooks and memories
41. Burgers and milkshakes
42. Swimming pools and fluffy towels
43. BBQ and fireworks
44. Daddies and daughters
45. Ocean breezes and open windows
46. Shampoo and conditioner

47. Tom and Jerry

48. Ben and Jerry
49. Ashton and Demi
50. Girlfriends and gossip
51. Easter and bunny
52. Oreos and milk
53. Pen and paper
54. Your kids and a day off

NEXT MONTH

Great wines–under $12

Is there a special list you'd like to see? Let us know at ghgoodlist@hearst.com.

PHOTOGRAPH BY WARNER BROS./NEAL PETERS COLLECTION

GIVEAWAY RULES

NO PURCHASE NECESSARY TO ENTER OR WIN

The following sweepstakes are open to legal U.S. residents (void in Puerto Rico) 18 and older, except employees of Hearst Communications, Inc., and Sponsors. Entries must be received by March 31, 2006. Winners will be selected at random on or about April 1, 2006.

To enter, mail a 3½- by 5½-inch postcard to: Good Housekeeping/[name of applicable sweepstakes], P.O. Box 1741, Sandusky, OH 44871-1741. You must include your name, address, and daytime phone number.

PRIZES

AquaTanica Spa Sweepstakes
(see page 63)

One hundred winners will be awarded one jar of AquaTanica Spa Sea Moisture Gel Soufflé (estimated retail value, $22.50).

Good Housekeeping Reader Sweepstakes
(see page 148)

Twelve winners will each receive one copy of Dana Buchman's book, *A Special Education* (estimated retail value, $21.95).

Cookies by Design Sweepstakes
(see page 202)

One hundred twenty-five winners will be awarded one gift certificate for a kit consisting of ten baked but undecorated daisy cookies, four bags of icing in spring colors, and edible decorations (estimated retail value, $25). Gift certificate is redeemable online at www.cookiesbydesign.com or at a company store and includes tax and shipping.

See www.goodhousekeeping.com for a complete list of sweepstakes rules.

For Mail Order Ad Rates, Write or Phone:
GOOD HOUSEKEEPING
DIRECT RESPONSE ADVERTISING
810 7th Avenue., New York, NY 10019
TARA TORINO (212) 649-2928
For Subscriptions Call: 1-800-888-7788
JUNE 2006 ISSUE CLOSES MARCH 15

Guaranteed Quality and service from America's premiere table pad company.
Free measuring service available in most areas. Satisfaction is guaranteed with return privilege. 30-year limited warranty.
1-800/328-7237 ext.240
www.sentrytablepad.com

Do you want to
Work at Home
and earn more money than in most office jobs?
Be a Medical Billing Specialist!
Get free facts! No cost! No obligation!
Call 1-800-388-8765, Dept. GHKA26,
or write **School of Medical Studies,** Dept. GHKA26, U.S. Career Institute, 2001 Lowe St., Ft. Collins, CO 80525 GL026

SPECIAL SCHOOL

A Special Choice for Special People

Progressive education, home community for the intellectually disabled child and adult. Opportunity for educational progress at any age—multiple educational, vocational, recreational and social activities. A year-round program with an active and full lifestyle among friends on an 850-acre bluegrass campus. Please write or call for brochure, or visit our web site.
STEWART HOME SCHOOL
4200 Lawrenceburg Road • Frankfort, KY 40601
John P. Stewart, M.D. • Phone 502-227-4821
www.stewarthome.com

Extra Thick. Extra Stick.
New Gorilla Tape sticks to things ordinary tapes simply can't.
1-800-966-3458 • www.gorillatape.com

words to live by

COMPILED BY KATIE HILBERT

Even if you're on the right track, you'll get run over if you just sit there.

WILL ROGERS

Life must be understood backward; but...it must be lived forward.

SØREN KIERKEGAARD

The most courageous act is still to think for yourself. Aloud.

COCO CHANEL

In the end it's not the years in your life that count. It's the life in your years.

ABRAHAM LINCOLN

secrets of a happy life

There are many ways of going forward, but only one way of standing still.

FRANKLIN D. ROOSEVELT

Shoot for the moon. Even if you miss, you'll land among the stars.

LES BROWN

I always say, "Don't make plans, make options."

JENNIFER ANISTON

You're braver than you believe, and stronger than you seem, and smarter than you think.

A.A. MILNE

There's something liberating about not pretending. Dare to embarrass yourself. Risk.

DREW BARRYMORE

One of the secrets of a happy life is continuous small treats.

IRIS MURDOCH

Getty Images

My Three Sons
Continued from page 54

told me that with three boys I'd be a good customer. He had boys. Windows have a tendency to break in their presence, he said.

I understand there are girls who play with trucks and cap guns, but they do so differently than boys. Other friends of ours have a girl who is one of the best kids at getting a fish on the line that I've ever seen. She flips her yellow locks behind her shoulders and then baits her own hook, casts her own line, lands the fish and dresses it out as well as any boy I know. We bring it back to the house for supper, but when it's almost done, she suggests I turn off the stove to allow the fish to finish cooking in the pan. Meanwhile, behind her our son pours a glass of milk, spilling half of it on the floor.

Last summer, during the long, bored days of August, our boys decided to put up a lemonade stand at the side of the road. As I watched them sitting in their chairs, teasing each other and laughing in the sun, it struck me that where it really matters, all children are essentially the same—they all like candy and a good book and to be swung through the air. They all can't wait for their birthdays. They bring out the best in us and then drive us halfway to crazy. They will take as much love as we can possibly pour into them. They are kids first, boys and girls second. Still, something tells me that Orphan Annie's lemonade stand wouldn't quite resemble the one our boys had put together.

Orphan Annie's lemonade stand would actually have lemonade. It would be cold, in a big glass pitcher and would strike the perfect balance between tart and sweet. There would be a neat stack of cookies on a plate directly in front of her. Chocolate chip and oatmeal raisin—big, moist and absolutely delicious.

My boys never actually got to the lemonade part of the lemonade stand. Instead, they raided our pantry and filled their table with cans of tuna and plastic bottles of Tums. The two oldest boys carefully lined individual Tums around each tuna can, and our youngest stacked piles of small cars on the corners of the table. After watching them do this, I called a neighbor to see if he could stop by on his way to work. "Bring some quarters," I told him. "And maybe some lemonade too." **FC**

Coming October 18

Special edition! Family Circle Christmas 2005

EASY RECIPES AND FRESH, SIMPLE IDEAS FOR THIS YEAR'S CELEBRATIONS

- 20 sweet treats that make the most of peppermint, pears and cranberries
- Ginger delights including a praline spice cake and a charming gingerbread chalet
- Jolly ways to deck the halls from top to bottom
- Helpful hints for wrapping anything and everything
- Illuminating design ideas that glitter and glow

Brian Hagiwara

Borders

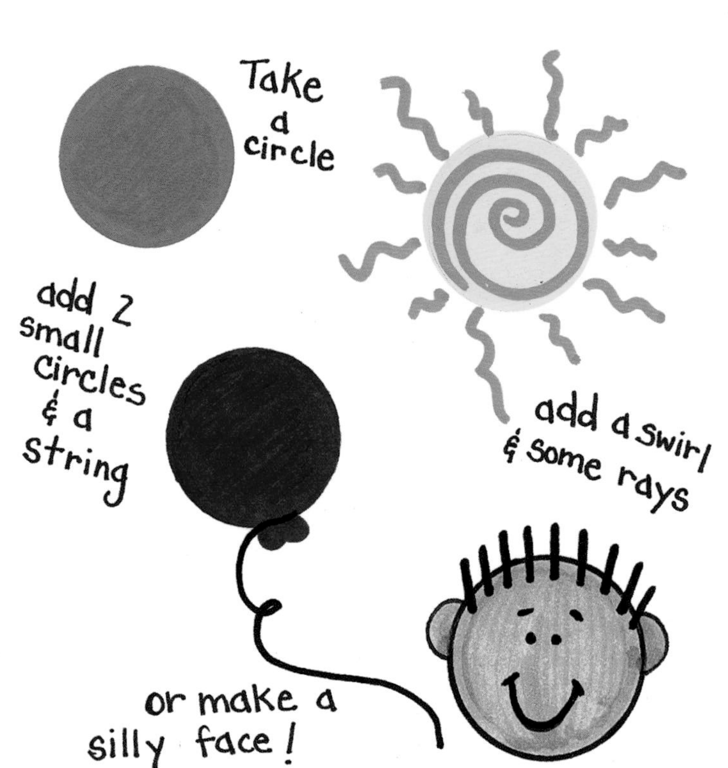

tips

1. Always work from top to bottom and left to right to prevent dragging your hand through a design you have just drawn.
2. For really straight borders, evenly space 2 strips of masking tape and draw the border between the strips.
3. If your pen tip gets into another color by accident, clean the tip by wiping it back and forth on a scrap piece of paper.
4. For small dots in a row, rest your hand on the table as you make the dots and pounce the pen in a row. If the ink stops flowing, push the pen tip down on scrap paper to re-ink the tip and then continue.

Teardrops
Step 1
Step 2
Hearts
Christmas Lights
Mouse
Carrot
Bunny
Butterfly
Fish
Step 1
Step 2
Step 3
BIRD
Flying Bird
Flowers

tips

1. Draw the outline of the teardrop and fill it in.

2. When making a larger heart, draw the heart then draw a teardrop highlight. Color around highlight. You can add a highlight later with white, but be sure the first color is completely dry.

3. Use a template to start your border then add your own designs. For the carrot border, I started with a large pinked edge template and then added the carrots.

Blobs, Blocks, & Shapes

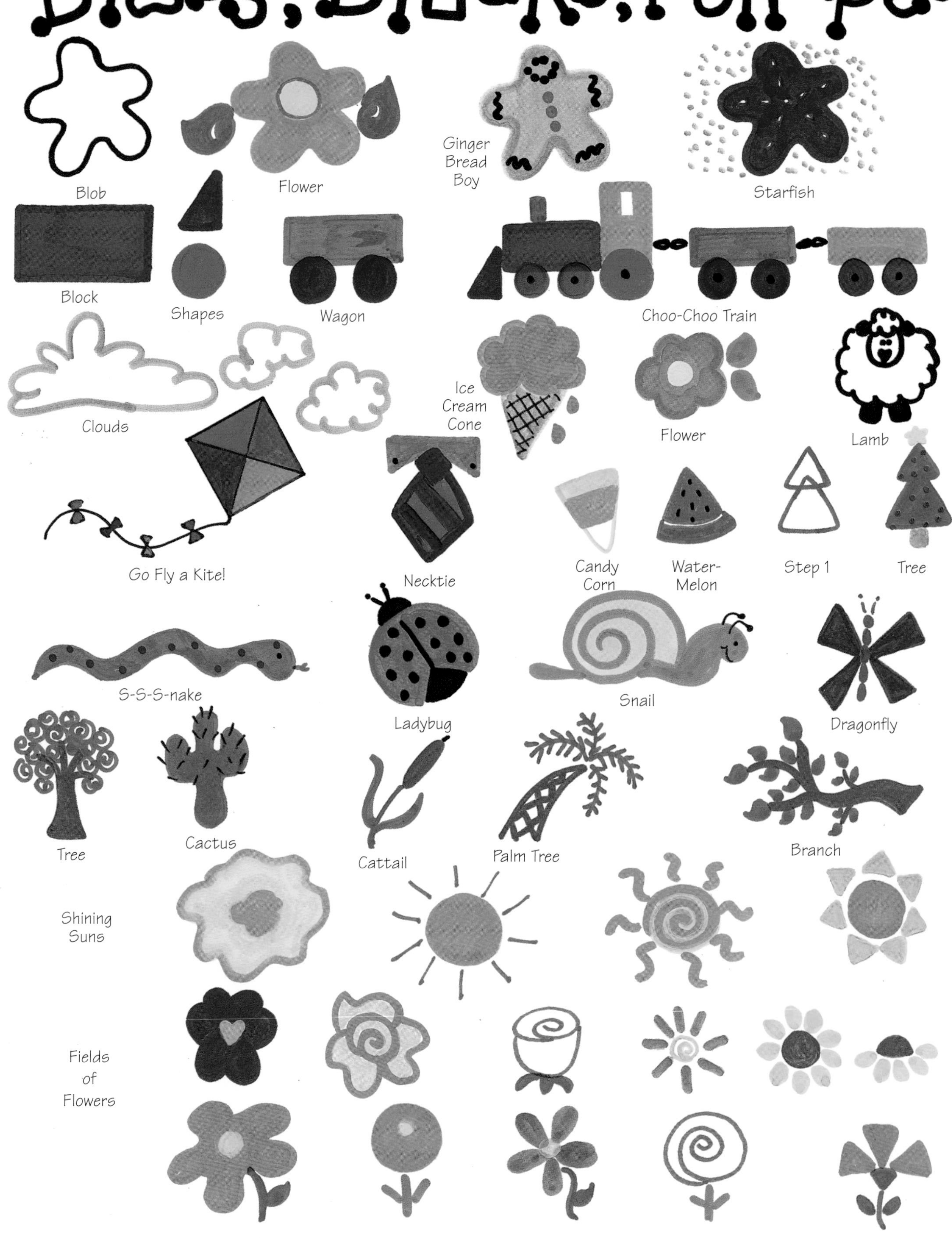

Apple
Butterfly
Cat
Dog
Easte r Egg
Fish
Golf Ball
House
Iris
Jack-O-Lantern
Kite
Lightbulb
Moon
Necktie
Owel
Puzzle
Piece
Question
Mark
Radish
Sun
Tree
Umbrella
Violet
Wagon
Xylophone
Yarn
Zebra

Faces & Figures
Start with a circle.
Use the letter "C" to add ears
add dots for eyes, a sideways "C" for mouth & circles for cheeks.
Faces
Butch
Suzy Q
Grandpa
Mother
Auntie Joan
Barbie
Hair
Mary Jo
Daddy
Grandma
Best Friends
BABY
Peggy
Holidays
Angel
Santa
Clown
Witch
Frankenstein
Jack-O-Lantern
Clothes
Shirt
Pants
1
2
Hat
Blouse
1
2
3
Bow
Dress
Shirt
People
Butch
Suzy Q
Grandma and Baby
Kitty Cat
Poochie Pup
25
Big Brother

Cheerleader
Football Player
45
2 Points
12
Basketball Player
Go team!
1
00
Baseball Player
Soccer Player
Ballerina
Flip-Over Freddie
Have fun!
Keep on Your toes!

Animals & bugs
Fido
Rover
Bowser
Spot
Fireplug
Pussy Cat
Tom Cat
Felix
Meow Kitty
Squeaky Mouse
Funny Bunny
Herby Hare
To make a bow draw a
Then add 2 ♡'s & fill in!
Teddy Bear
Bow-Wow
Moo-Moo
Mrs. Chicken
Baa-Baa Blue Sheep
Piggle Wiggle
A Horse is a Horse, of Course

Leo the Lion
Tommy the Tiger
Elmo the Elephant
Polly the Parrot
George the Giraffe
Albert the Alligator
Clyde the Camel
Herbert the Hippo

Kevin
Timmy's
School Box
AMY
'98
Baby
Tom
Jan
Amy
Sue
John
Happy Holidays
from the
Hansen's
Suzane
Jan
Ed
Cyndi
Tom
Sharon
Amy
April
Tim
Kevin
Krisy
Sports Mom
Amy

PAINT

PERSONALIZE

Just Decorate any item as a Personalized Gift!

to Decorate:

• CERAMICS • **PLASTIC** • GLASS •
• METAL • **WOOD** • PAPER •

1. For ease in drawing a design on plastic, make a black and white photocopy of your design and tape it behind your project. Then just trace over the design with desired pens.

2. If you make a mistake on your project you can clean it off with mineral spirits and a cotton swab. Always test mineral spirits in an inconspicuous place first to make sure it won't harm the plastic.

Fall & Halloween
Step 1
Step 2
Step 3
WITCH
Step 1
Step 2
PUMPKIN
Jack-O-Lantern
Step 1
Step 2
Step 3
CAT
Happy Halloween!

Spring & Easter
Step 1
Step 2
Step 3
EASTER BASKET
Step 1
Step 2
Step 3
Step 4
EASTER BUNNY
Step 1
Step 2
Step 3
CHICK
Happy Spring!

Christmas
Step 1
Step 2
Step 3
CHRISTMAS MOOSE
Step 1
Step 2
Step 3
SNOWMAN
Happy
Holidays

Babies

Girl Baby

Rattle

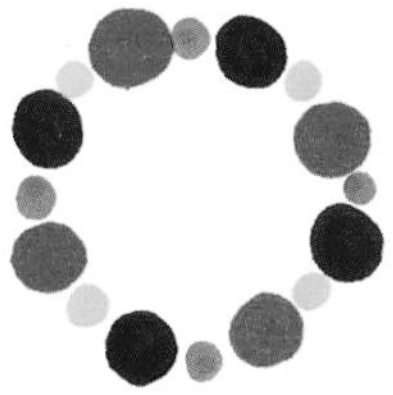

Teething Ring

Buggy

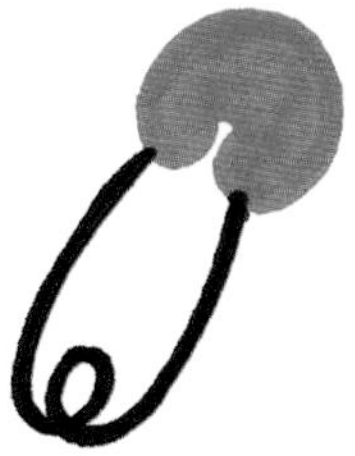

Girl's Diaper Pin

Boy's Diaper Pin

Ducky

Sailboat

Moon and Stars

Boy Baby

Bottle

Pacifier

Baby

Teddy Bear

Bib

It's a Boy!

It's a girl!

Dinosaurs

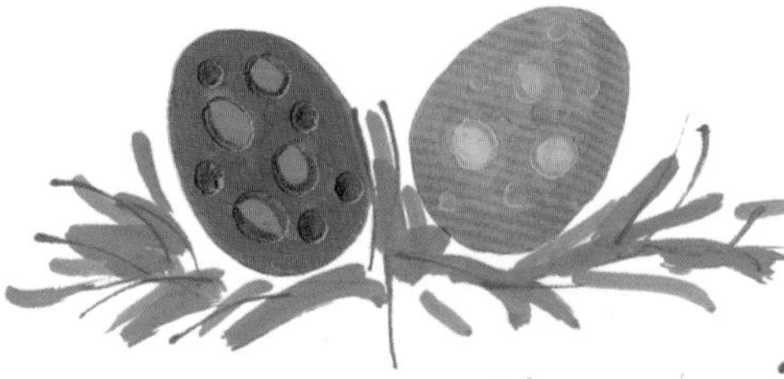

Dan Diplodocus

Terry Tyranosaurus

Polly Polacanthus

Teresa Pterodactyl

Tony Triceratops

FARM FUN
Step 1
Step 2
Step 3
SCARECROW
Charlene Chicken
Pauline Pig
Lester Lamb
Dilbert Duck
Caroline Cow
Roosevelt Rooster
Little Green Tractor
Little Red Barn

Sealife
Step 1
Step 2
COCONUT PALM
Step 1
SEAWEED
Float
Sand Castle
Sun Glasses
Seashells
Oscar
Octopus
Sammy
Shark
Star-
fish
Sea
Snail
Lucy
Lobster
Sylvester
Seahorse
Coral

Snakes, Bugs & Lizards
S-s-s-s-s-s-linky S-s-s-s-s-s-nakes
Samantha Sea Serpent
Wally Wasp
Darlene Dragonfly
Isador Insect
Baxter Bug
Katy Caterpillar
Splendora Spider
Tommy Turtle
Lester Lizard
Gertrude Gecko

Cats
Cat, cats and more cats are just a few simple steps away.
Step 1
Step 2
Step 3
CAT

Dogs
Step 1
Step 2
Step 3
Step 4
DOG
Man's best friend! Follow the steps shown to make all kinds of canine creations.
DOG

Birds
Step 1
Step 2
Step 3
BLUEBIRD
Samuel
Seagull
Daphne Dove
Sebastian Swan
Hooty Owl
Felicity
Flamingo
Thomas
Toucan
Terrance
Turkey

Transportation
Tricycle
Wagon
Car
Police Car
Taxi
Convertible
Highways and Roads
Ocean Liner
Sailboat
Ark
Helicopter
Airplane
Jet
Pickup Truck
Motorcycle
BUS
School Bus
MILK
Dump Truck
Milk Truck
Fire Truck

School & Sports
HISTORY
MATH
Pencil
Crayon
Scissors
Ruler
Artist Palette
Artist Brush
Football
GO
Hockey Puck
Ice Skates
Hockey Stick
Pennant
Football Helmet
Megaphone
Pompom
Basketball
Jersey
00
Glove
Baseball
Bat
Golf Ball
Golf Clubs and Bag
Soccer Ball
Soccer Cleats
School